What comes next?

Bobbie Kalman

Crabtree Publishing Company
www.crabtreebooks.com

Created by Bobbie Kalman

For Reagan Miller, with much thanks.
I couldn't have done these books without your help!

Author and Editor-in-Chief
Bobbie Kalman

Editors
Reagan Miller
Robin Johnson

Photo research
Crystal Sikkens

Design
Bobbie Kalman
Katherine Kantor
Samantha Crabtree (cover)

Production coordinator
Katherine Kantor

Illustrations
Barbara Bedell: pages 15, 23

Photographs
© BigStockPhoto.com: page 19 (tree frog)
© Dreamstime.com: page 1 (frog)
© iStockphoto.com: page 4
© 2008 Jupiterimages Corporation: pages 18 (bottom left), 23 (arctic fox)
© ShutterStock.com: cover, pages 1 (background), 3, 5, 6, 7, 8, 9, 10, 11, 12, 13, 14, 15, 16, 17, 18 (all except bottom left), 19 (all except tree frog), 20, 21, 22 (all except dog and horse), 23 (all except arctic fox), 24 (all except dog and horse)
Other images by Photodisc

Library and Archives Canada Cataloguing in Publication

Kalman, Bobbie, 1947-
   What comes next? / Bobbie Kalman.

(Looking at nature)
Includes index.
ISBN 978-0-7787-3319-5 (bound).--ISBN 978-0-7787-3339-3 (pbk.)

   1. Pattern perception--Juvenile literature. I. Title.
II. Series: Looking at nature (St. Catharines, Ont.)

BF294.K35 2007   j152.14'23   C2007-904735-1

Library of Congress Cataloging-in-Publication Data

Kalman, Bobbie.
   What comes next? / Bobbie Kalman.
       p. cm. -- (Looking at nature)
   Includes index.
   ISBN-13: 978-0-7787-3319-5 (rlb)
   ISBN-10: 0-7787-3319-X (rlb)
   ISBN-13: 978-0-7787-3339-3 (pb)
   ISBN-10: 0-7787-3339-4 (pb)
   1. Visual perception--Juvenile literature. 2. Pattern perception--Juvenile literature. I. Title. II. Series.

BF241.K35 2008
153.7'5--dc22
                                                       2007030366

Crabtree Publishing Company

www.crabtreebooks.com   1-800-387-7650

Copyright © **2008 CRABTREE PUBLISHING COMPANY.** All rights reserved. No part of this publication may be reproduced, stored in a retrieval system or be transmitted in any form or by any means, electronic, mechanical, photocopying, recording, or otherwise, without the prior written permission of Crabtree Publishing Company. In Canada: We acknowledge the financial support of the Government of Canada through the Book Publishing Industry Development Program (BPIDP) for our publishing activities.

Published in Canada
Crabtree Publishing
616 Welland Ave.
St. Catharines, Ontario
L2M 5V6

Published in the United States
Crabtree Publishing
PMB16A
350 Fifth Ave., Suite 3308
New York, NY 10118

Published in the United Kingdom
Crabtree Publishing
White Cross Mills
High Town, Lancaster
LA1 4XS

Published in Australia
Crabtree Publishing
386 Mt. Alexander Rd.
Ascot Vale (Melbourne)
VIC 3032

Contents

What comes next?	4
Which color?	6
How many parts?	8
Big and small	10
Which set is next?	12
Which season is it?	14
Animals in winter	16
How will they look?	18
Big changes!	20
Answers to questions	22
Words to know and Index	24

What comes next?

This book asks you to look closely at some pictures. Think about what you see. Then answer the questions. Can you guess what comes next?

In this picture, a mouse is sitting on a cat.

In the picture above, a cat is sitting on a dog.
In the picture below, there is a dog and a horse.
What do you think comes next? If you do not
know, turn to page
22 for the answer.

Which color?

Look at the rainbow on this page. The colors of a rainbow are red, orange, yellow, green, blue, and purple.

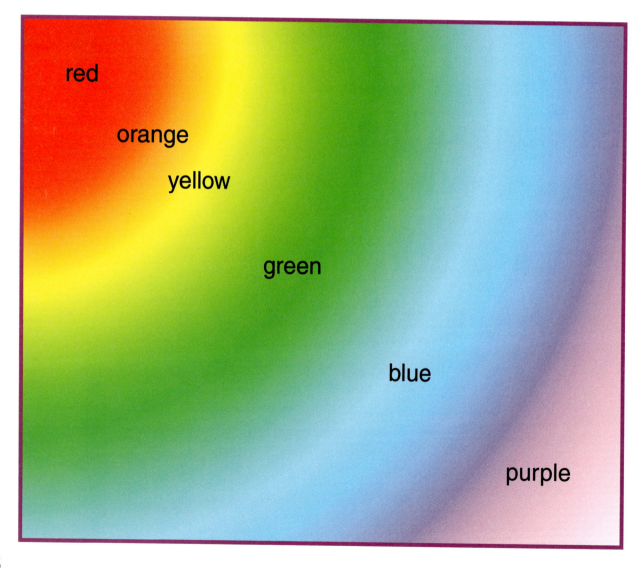

This flower has three rainbow colors. Which colors are they?

Is the next rainbow color on this lizard or on this fish?

How many parts?

Some things are made up of parts. A snail has one foot. How many wings does a bat have?

foot

bat

Big and small

elephant

Look at the animals on this page. The elephant is the biggest. Which animal is the next biggest?

tiger

hippo

Is the tiger the second biggest animal, or is the hippo next in size?

mouse

rat

Which is the smallest animal on this page? Which is the biggest? Put the animals in order from smallest to biggest.

dog

kitten

Which set is next?

These three chicks make a **set**. This set of chicks has two yellow chicks and a black chick in the middle.

How many chicks are in set two?

How is set two different from set one?

How are the chicks in set three the same as the chicks in set one? How are they different?

Which set comes next? Is it set four or set five?

Which season is it?

Many people live in places where there are four **seasons**. The four seasons are winter, spring, summer, and fall. Which season is shown in each of these pictures?

In which season can flowers grow because there is no more snow?

In this season, I go to the beach to swim and play. I do not go to school.

In this season, I dress in warm clothes. I like to ski on fresh snow.

When do leaves fall from the trees? Can you name this season, please?

Animals in winter

Animals that live in places with four seasons have to keep warm during winter. Some animals have long winter naps. Some animals grow thick fur or feathers. Some animals go to warmer places in the fall. They come back home in the spring.

1. What do ground squirrels do in winter?
2. Do Canada geese sleep all winter? What comes next for these animals?
3. What happens to the arctic fox when the weather turns very cold?

How will they look?

Animals are **living things**. Living things grow and change. These baby animals will change as they grow up. How will each baby on this page look when it is fully grown? Look at the animals on page 19!

Match each baby animal on page 18 with the correct **adult** animal on this page. An adult animal is fully grown.

Big changes!

This picture shows the changes in the life of a monarch butterfly. A monarch butterfly starts its life inside an egg. When it comes out of the egg, it is a **caterpillar**. The caterpillar grows. It then hangs from a tree and makes a hard shell around itself. The shell is called a **chrysalis**. A monarch butterfly comes out of the chrysalis.

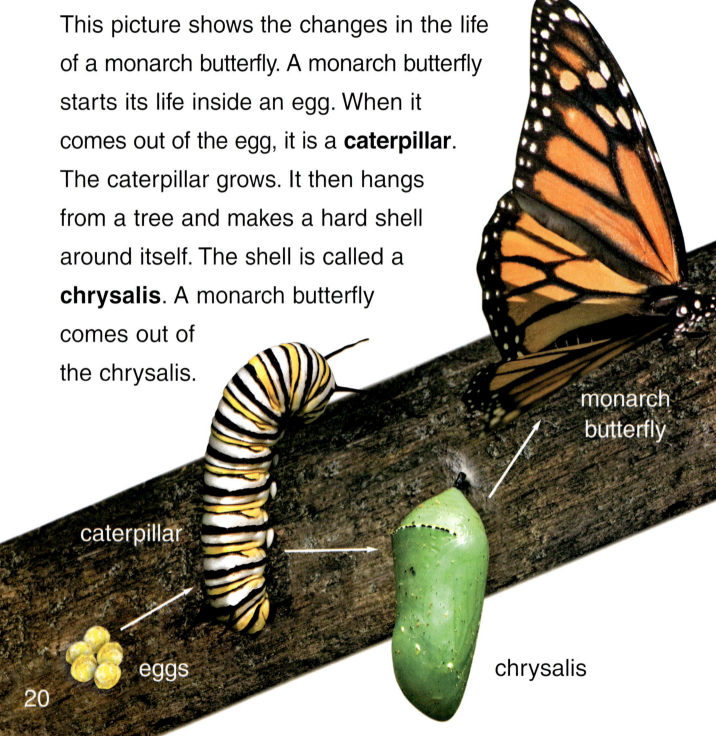

monarch butterfly

caterpillar

eggs

chrysalis

1. How has the chrysalis changed? Look at the one on page 20.
2. Why does the butterfly have to wait after it comes out of the chrysalis?
3. What does it do next? See page 23!

chrysalis

Answers to questions

These pages show what came next. Here are the answers to the questions in the book.

Page 3

This girl has a big stack of books. What comes next? The books fall down!

Page 5

A mouse is on a cat. A cat is on a dog. What comes next? A dog climbs on a horse, of course!

Page 7

The colors in the flower are red, orange, and yellow. The lizard is green. Its color comes next in the rainbow.

Page 9

The deer has four legs. It comes after the clover, which has three leaves.

Page 10

The hippo is the second biggest animal.

Page 11

The order from smallest to biggest is mouse, rat, kitten, and dog.

Pages 12-13

The next set of chicks is set four.

Pages 14-15

The seasons in the pictures are spring, summer, winter, and fall.

Pages 18-19

The matching babies and adults are 1-C, 2-B, 3-A, and 4-D.

Pages 16-17

1. Ground squirrels sleep all winter.
2. Canada geese fly to warmer places.
3. Arctic foxes grow thick white fur.

geese

arctic fox

Pages 20-21

1. The chrysalis has become clear.
2. The butterfly's wings are wet when it comes out of the chrysalis. The butterfly must wait for its wings to dry before it can fly.
3. The butterfly flies away.

Words to know and Index

animals
pages 10, 11, 16, 17, 18, 19, 23

adult animals
pages 19, 23

answers
pages 5, 22-23

baby animals
pages 18, 19, 23

big
pages 10-11, 23

butterfly changes
pages 20-21, 23

colors
pages 6-7, 22

parts
pages 8-9

seasons
pages 14-15, 16, 23

sets
pages 12-13, 23

small
pages 10-11, 23

Printed in the U.S.A.